8.95

INTERIM SITE

x629.46 Baker.D

Baker, David, 1944-

Observing the earth

Stepping Into Space

OBSERVING THE EARTH

by David Baker

THE AUTHOR — David Baker PhD, has been actively involved with NASA in the planning of the US space program. He has contributed to numerous aerospace and defense journals, and has written several books on space related subjects. Dr. Baker advises Independent Television News on American space operations and makes frequent TV appearances. He currently heads a consultant firm in space business development.

© 1986 Rourke Enterprises, Inc.

All rights reserved. No part of this book may be reproduced or utilized in any form or by any means, electronic or mechanical including photocopying, recording or by any information storage and retrieval system without permission in writing from the publisher.

EVANSTON PUBLIC LIBRARY
CHILDREN'S DEPARTMENT
1703 ORRINGTON AVENUE
EVANSTON, ILLINOIS 60201

Library of Congress Cataloging in Publication Data

Baker, David, 1944-
  Observing the earth.

  (Stepping into space)
  Summary: Discusses how satellites of various types observe and record earth conditions, thus providing data to meteorologists, farmers, ship owners, and others so they can make informed decisions.
  1. Meteorological satellites—Juvenile literature. 2. Landsat satellites—Juvenile literature. 3. Remote sensing—Juvenile literature. [1. Artificial satellites] I. Title. II. Series: Baker, David, 1944- Stepping into space.
  TL798.M4B28   1986   621.36'78   86-21937
  ISBN 0-86592-974-2

Rourke Enterprises, Inc.
Vero Beach, FL 32964

Scientists watch the weather for several reasons. They want to forecast conditions a few hours or days ahead and study the way storms develop. If possible they may wish to change the weather. The science of weather watching is called meteorology. Before satellites, meteorologists could send up only balloons and airplanes to gain weather information.

Satellites help weathermen study the weather ▶

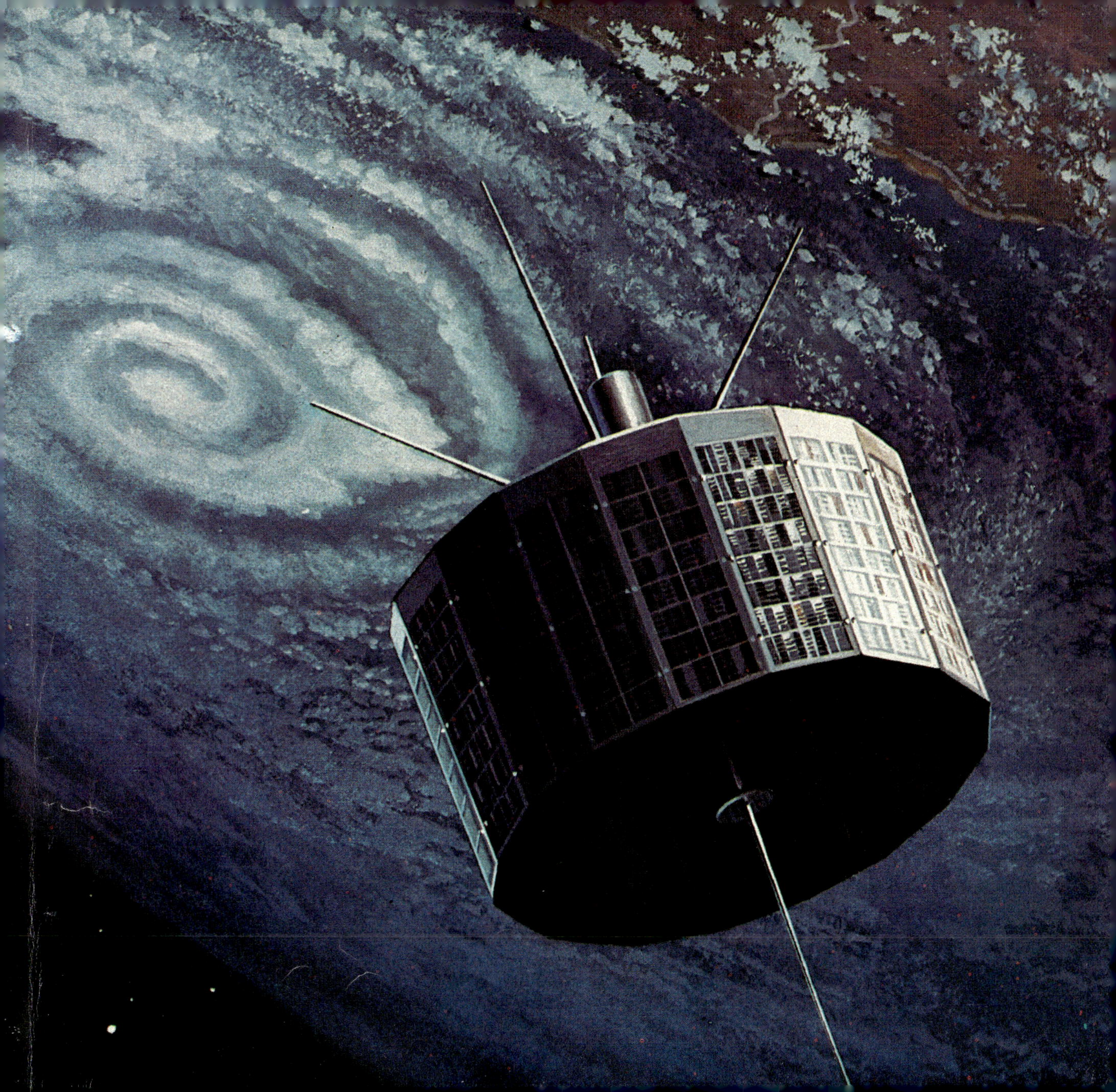

Now they use instruments aboard spaceships to constantly watch the atmosphere. Satellites help weathermen to better understand what other instruments tell them. Weather observation is not the only use for "earth watching" satellites.

Instruments, carried on satellites in space, watch the weather day and night ▶

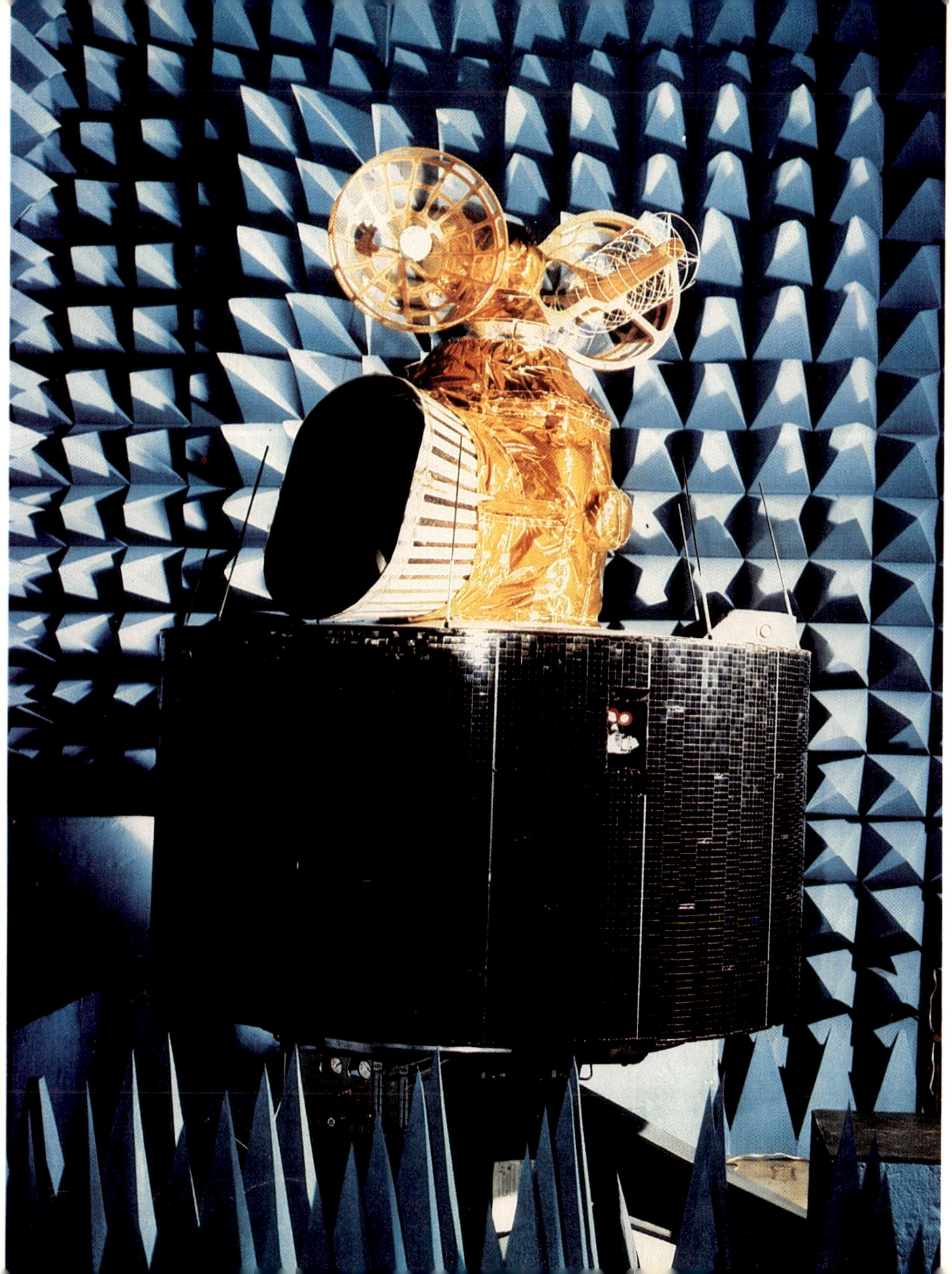

Satellites also help protect farm crops, range land and forests. These satellites are called "remote sensing" satellites. They have many instruments used to observe the earth from a distance. They are far from the earth's surface and rely on observation, not touch or direct measurement, to record what they see.

Special satellites used for taking pictures of the earth help scientists understand what is happening at the surface ▶

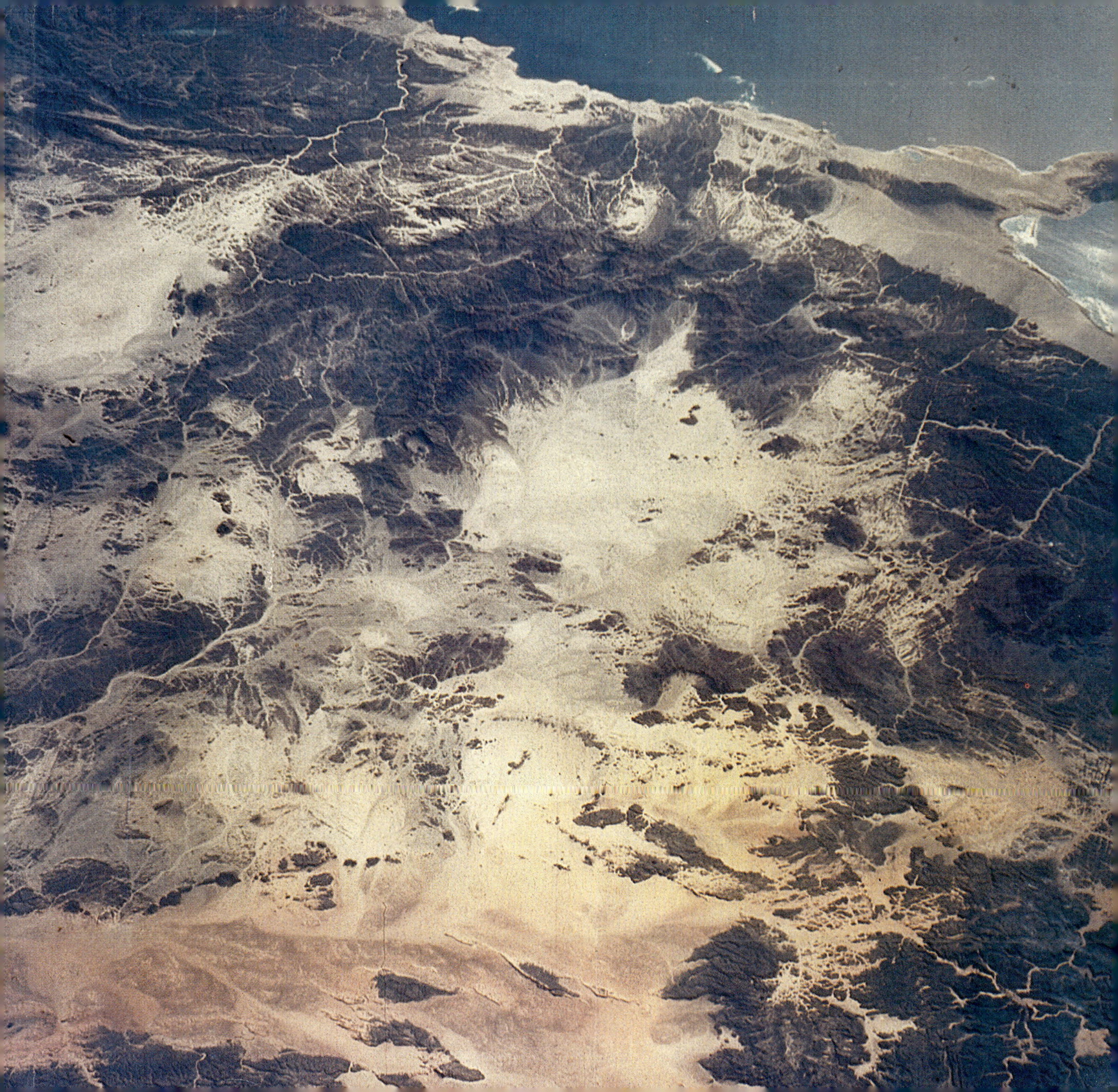

There are two types of weather satellites. The first kind is placed in a path that carries it over both North and South Poles. In this type of orbit the satellite goes around and around the earth, taking pictures of the weather as the planet spins beneath it.

Satellites in polar orbit keep watch on the weather below ▶

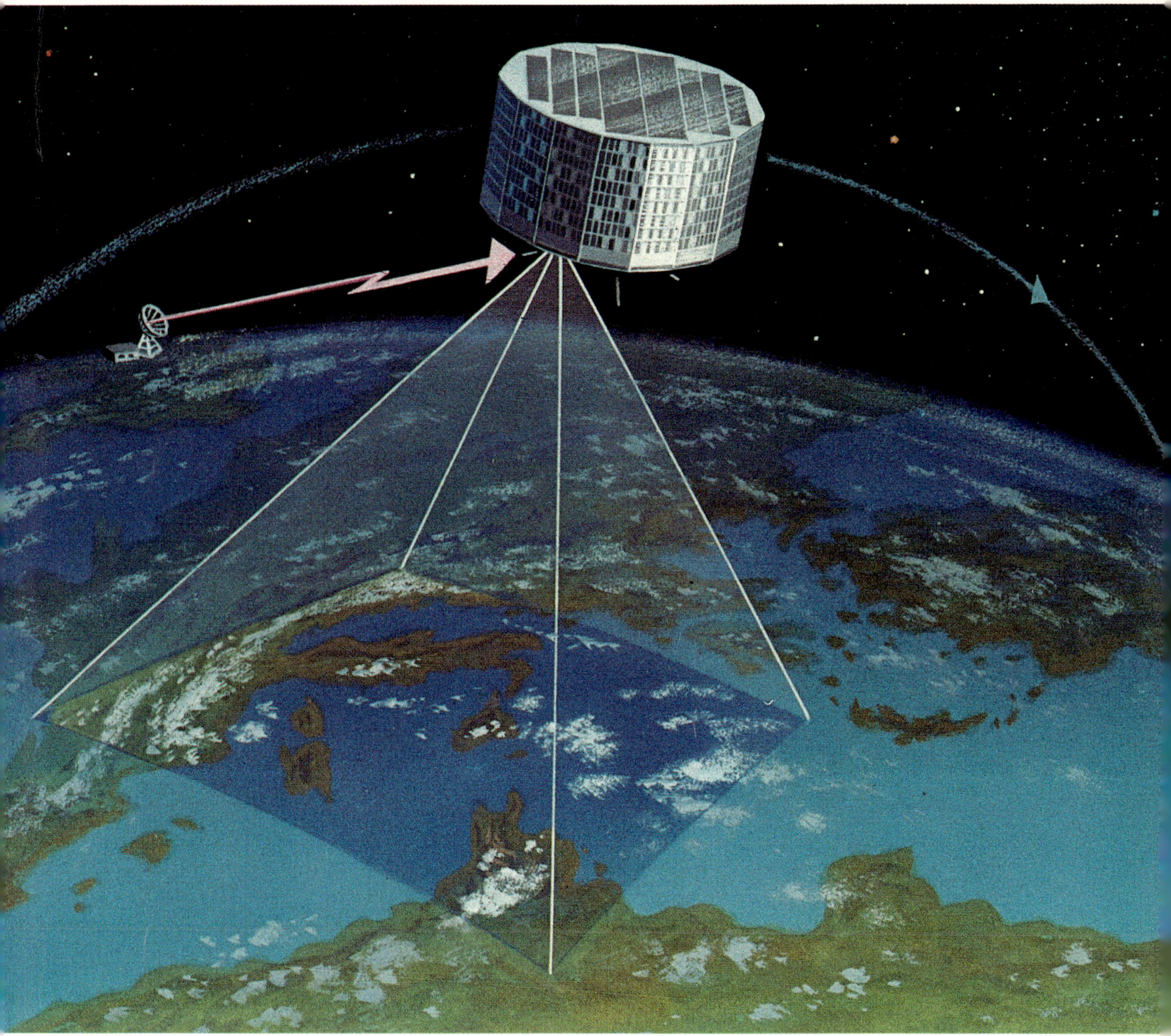

The second kind of weather satellite is placed in orbit 22,300 miles high. From this position it can see almost half the globe. It appears to remain fixed in one position because the orbiting satellite keeps pace with the movement of the ground below. That is why it is called a geostationary orbit. The satellite in polar orbit is only 450 miles above the earth and takes pictures over the same area at a fixed time each day. The satellite high above earth continually takes pictures of weather systems across wide areas.

Satellites in stationary orbit get a complete view of one half of the earth ▶

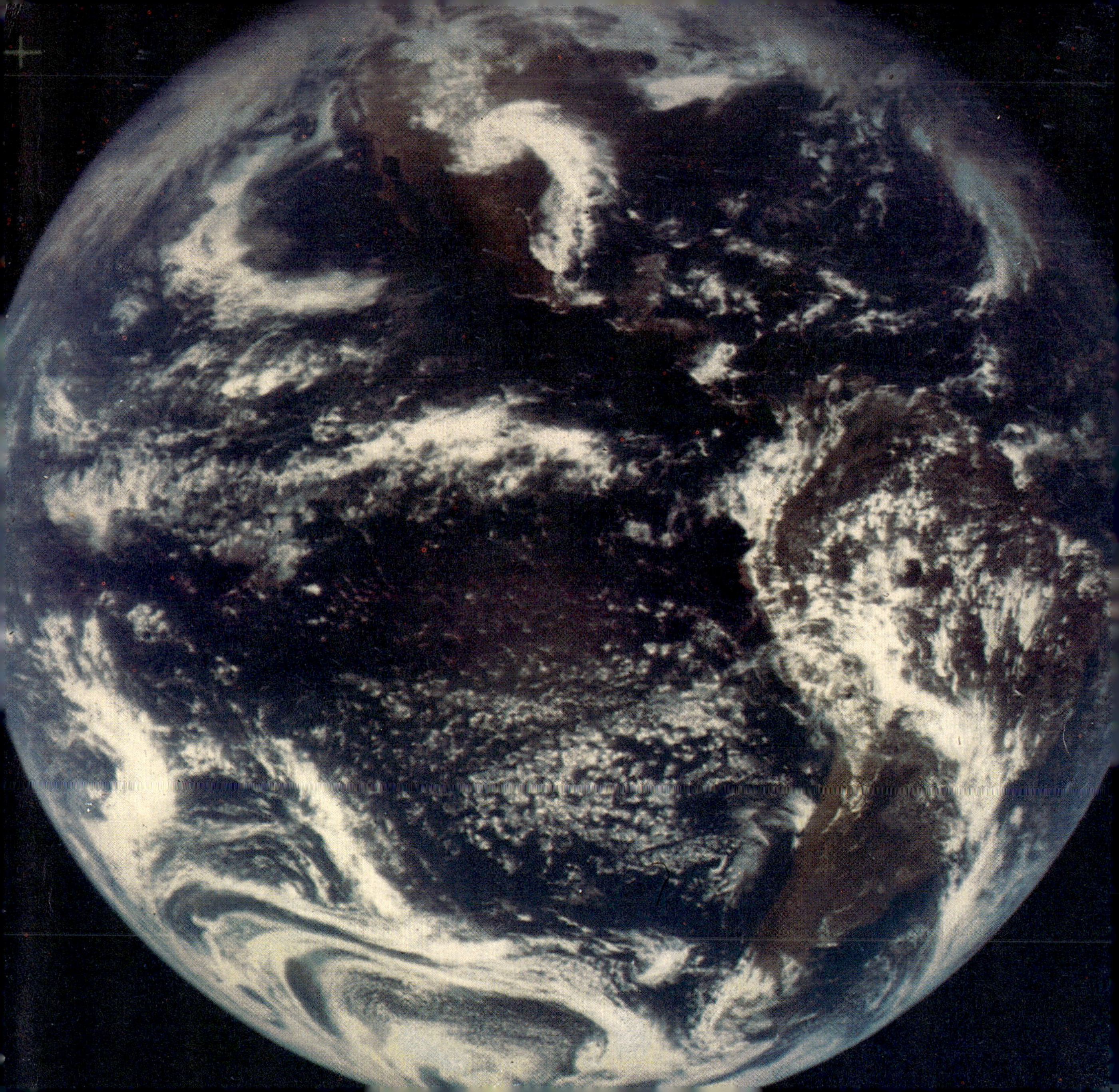

United States weather satellites are owned by the National Oceanic and Atmospheric Administration, or NOAA for short. The information they provide is used for weather forecasting. It also helps track hurricanes, watch for changes in the health of crops, and rescue stranded people. The low orbit satellites can pick up radio signals from people in trouble. They can tell rescue services the place from which the call is coming. Each weather satellite carries special instruments to measure the atmosphere. Meterologists get information about the amount of water in clouds and about the different levels of temperature.

Violent events like hurricanes are continually tracked by US weather satellites ▶

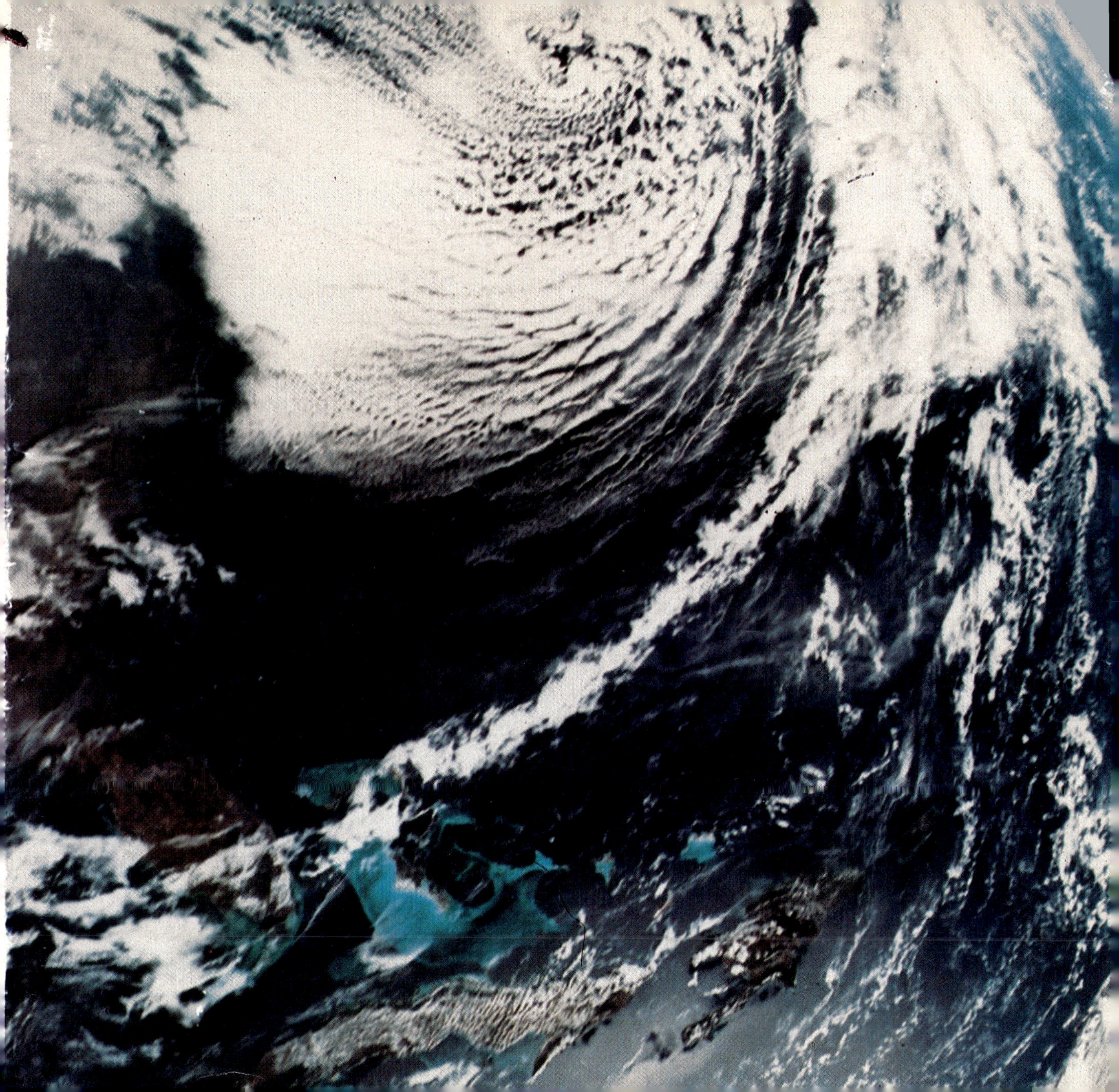

All this is done by remote sensing. This information, called "data", is picked up by different stations around the nation. Other instruments on the ground and in the air help develop a picture of the weather. Some instruments send their data to the satellite which then sends it to the weather station. In this way the satellites are data collection platforms.

Weather satellites like this take pictures in strips ▶

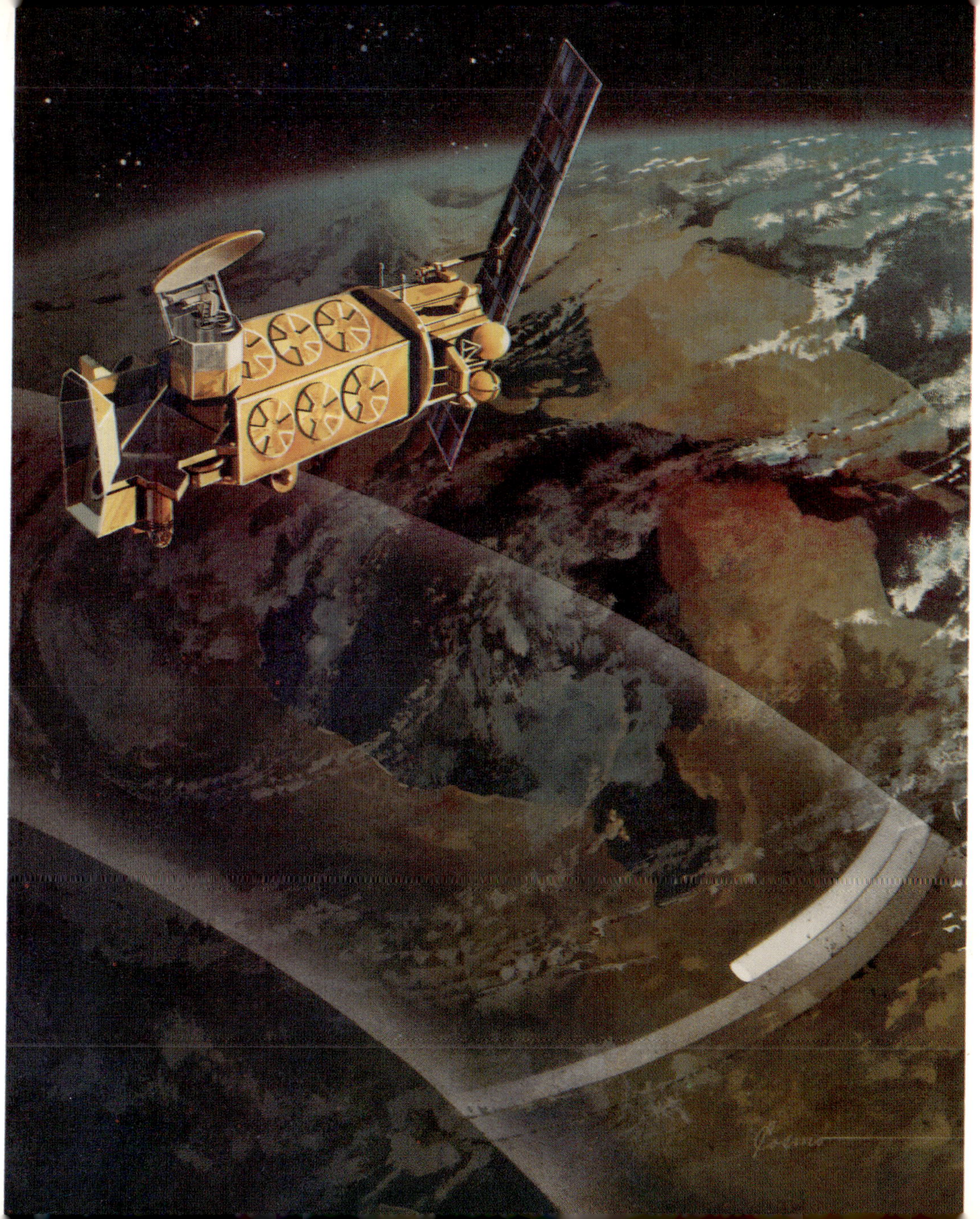

Satellites have been helping US weathermen since the first satellite was launched in 1960. Since 1972, another type of earth watching satellite has been helping farmers, fishermen and the people who design our cities. The satellite Landsat looks at the earth with special cameras. Ordinary photographs hide a lot of detail the human eye cannot see.

Landsat was the world's first remote sensing satellite, launched by NASA in 1972 ▶

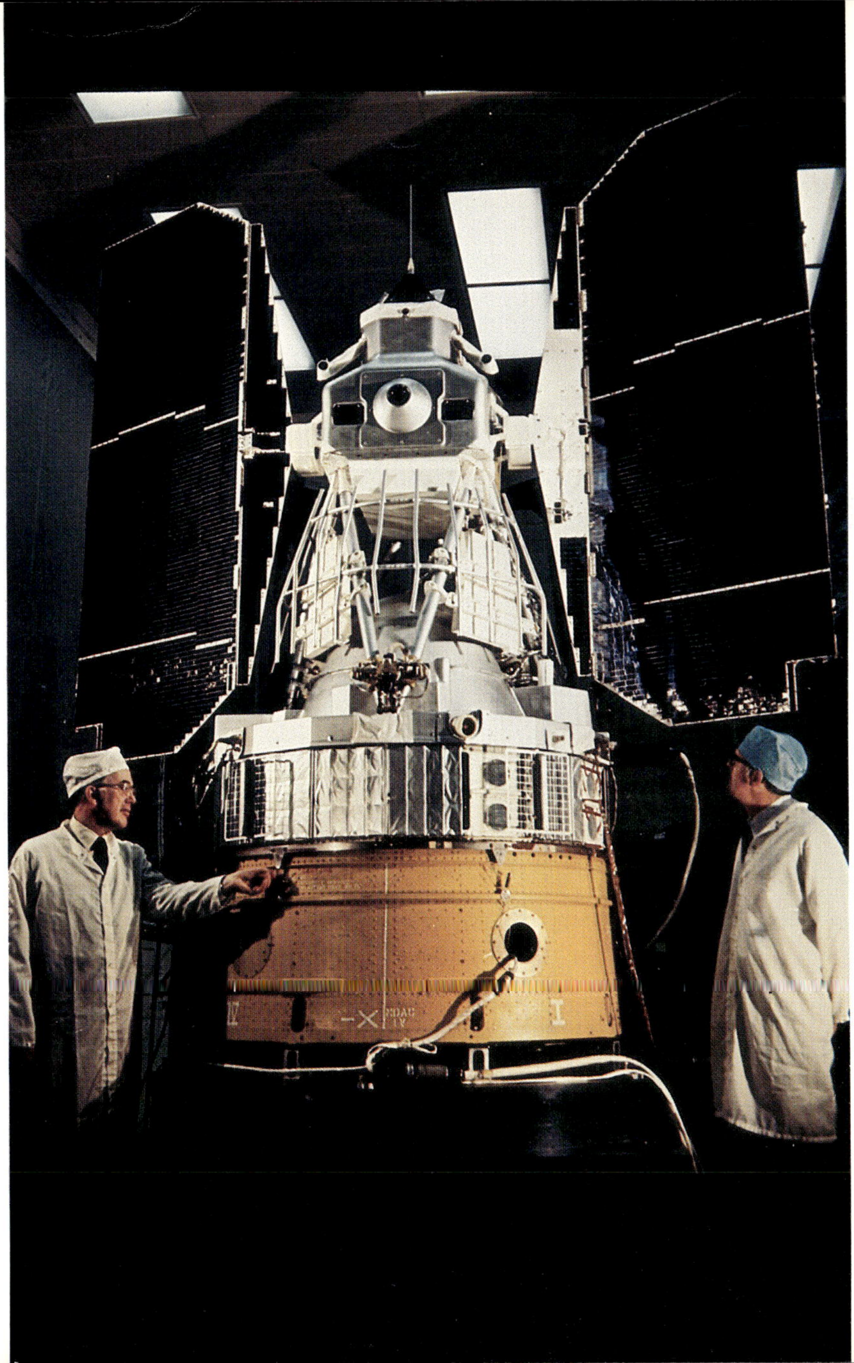

A camera which takes several pictures of the same area in different colors can show that detail. This helps people find new oil fields and metals for industry. Special methods are used to put the different color pictures together. The pictures show things no eye or ordinary camera would see. The Landsat satellite goes around the earth at a height of 440 miles. It is in polar orbit and takes pictures over the same spot on the ground every sixteen days.

Like weather satellites in polar orbit, Landsat views the earth over the same ▶
spot every sixteen days

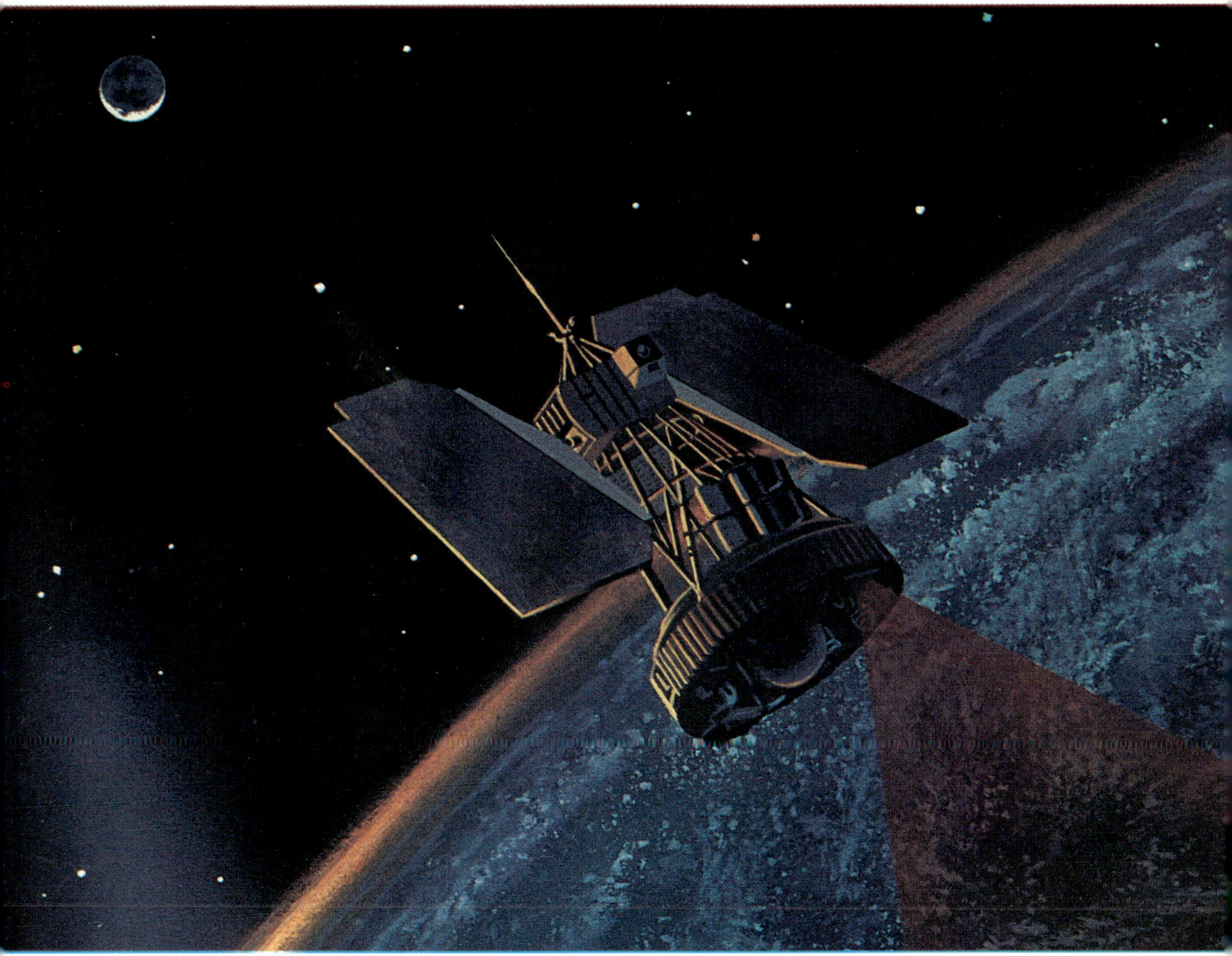

Landsat satellites provide information useful to many different people. Farmers receive warning of a crop disease before it becomes visible on the ground. Fishermen are helped with information about where the fish are and what the ocean life is doing. People looking after forests keep count of trees with Landsat data.

Sea conditions and schools of fish can be seen from space ▶

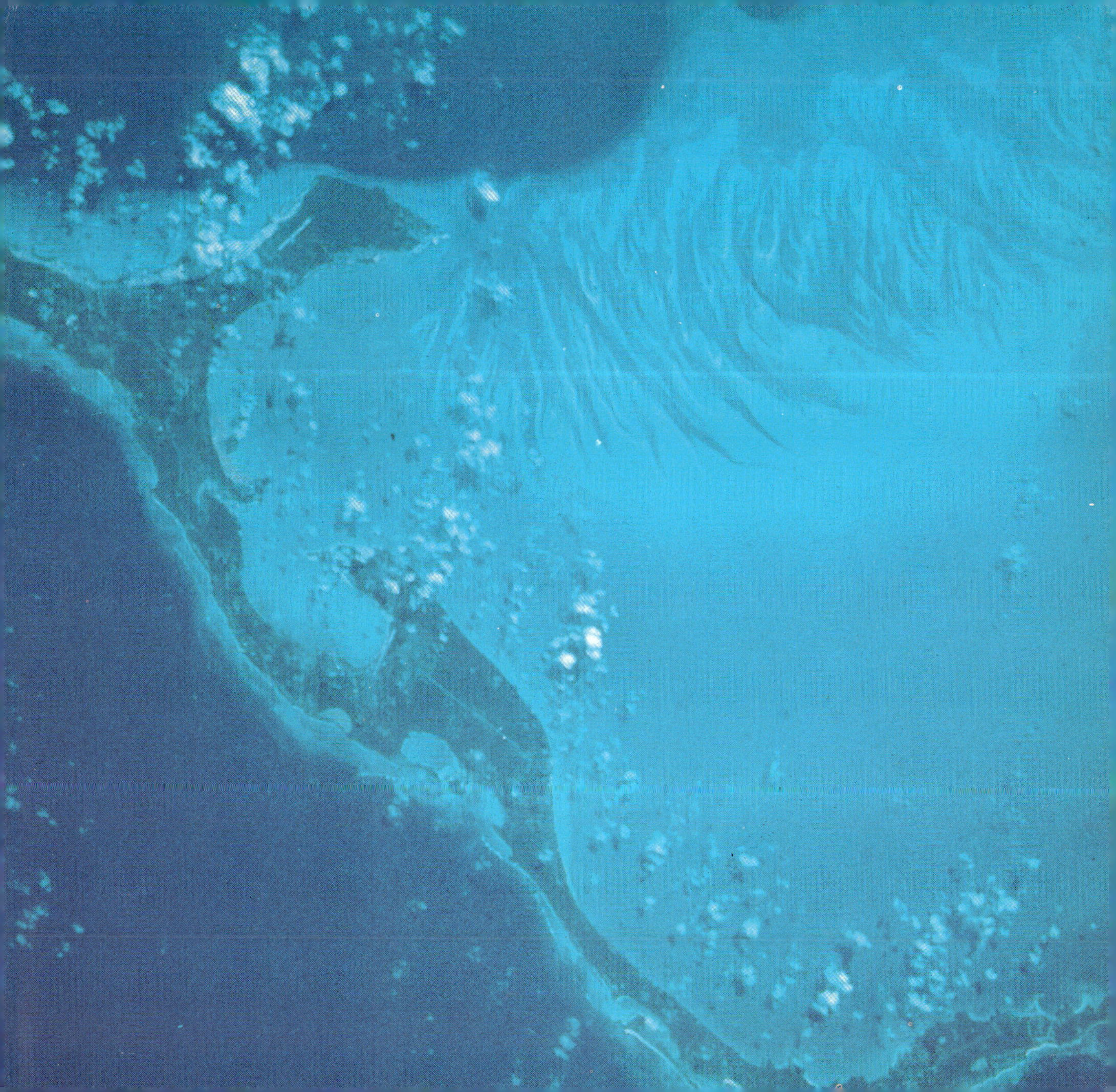

Water is important for all of us. It is necessary to keep watch on water levels in resevoirs. Landsat helps do that. People who build freeways and new towns watch how their plans affect the surroundings.

Views of different weather systems help give warnings about tropical storms ▶

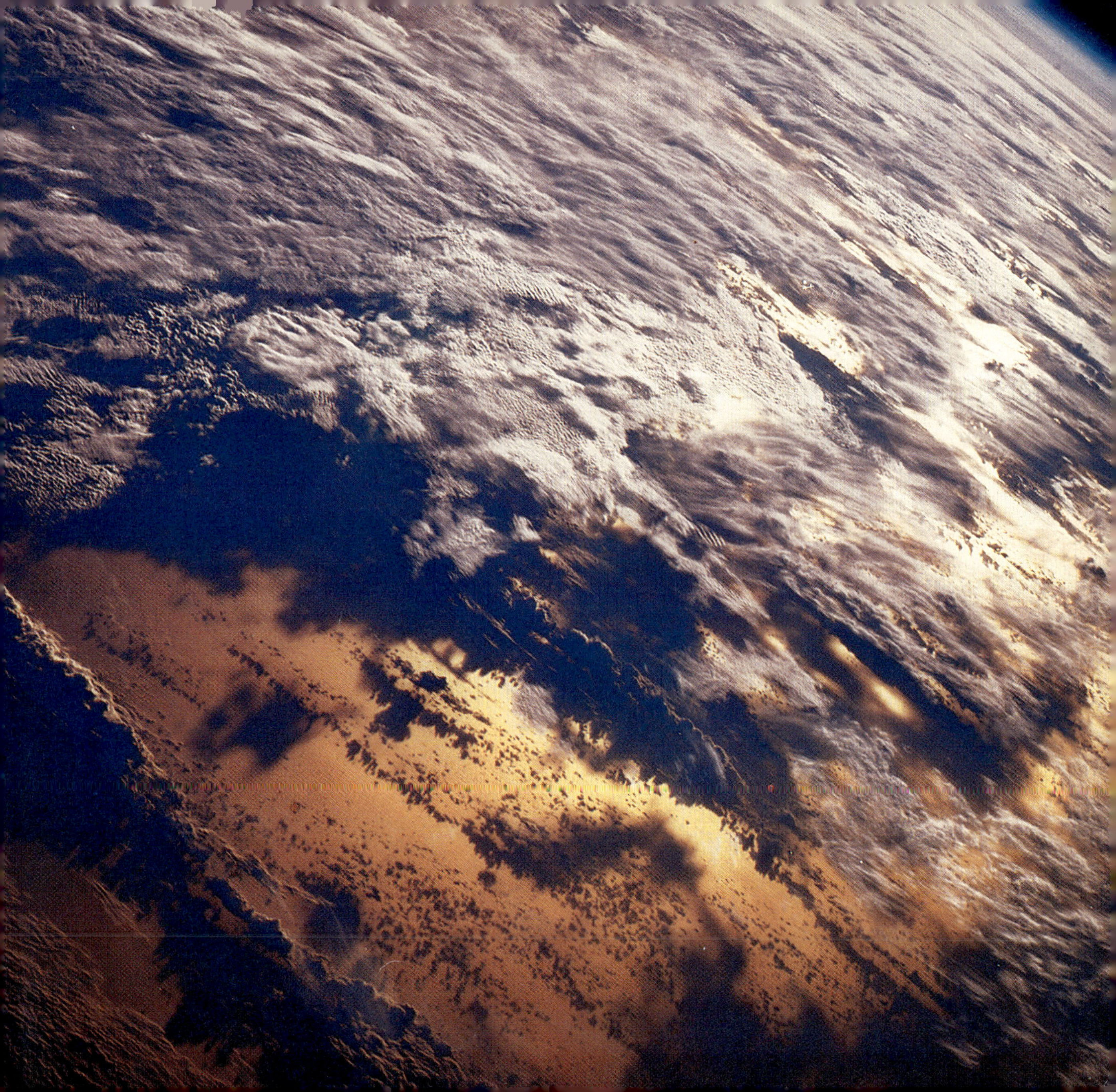

Architects who add developments to big cities also use Landsat. The satellite can track oil or refuse in rivers. It can also spot air pollution from factories. Many people in different jobs get help from Landsat satellites. The United States has allowed farmers in other countries to use the Landsat. Healthier crops and better harvests are the results worldwide.

A view of the NASA Kennedy Space Center in Florida ▶

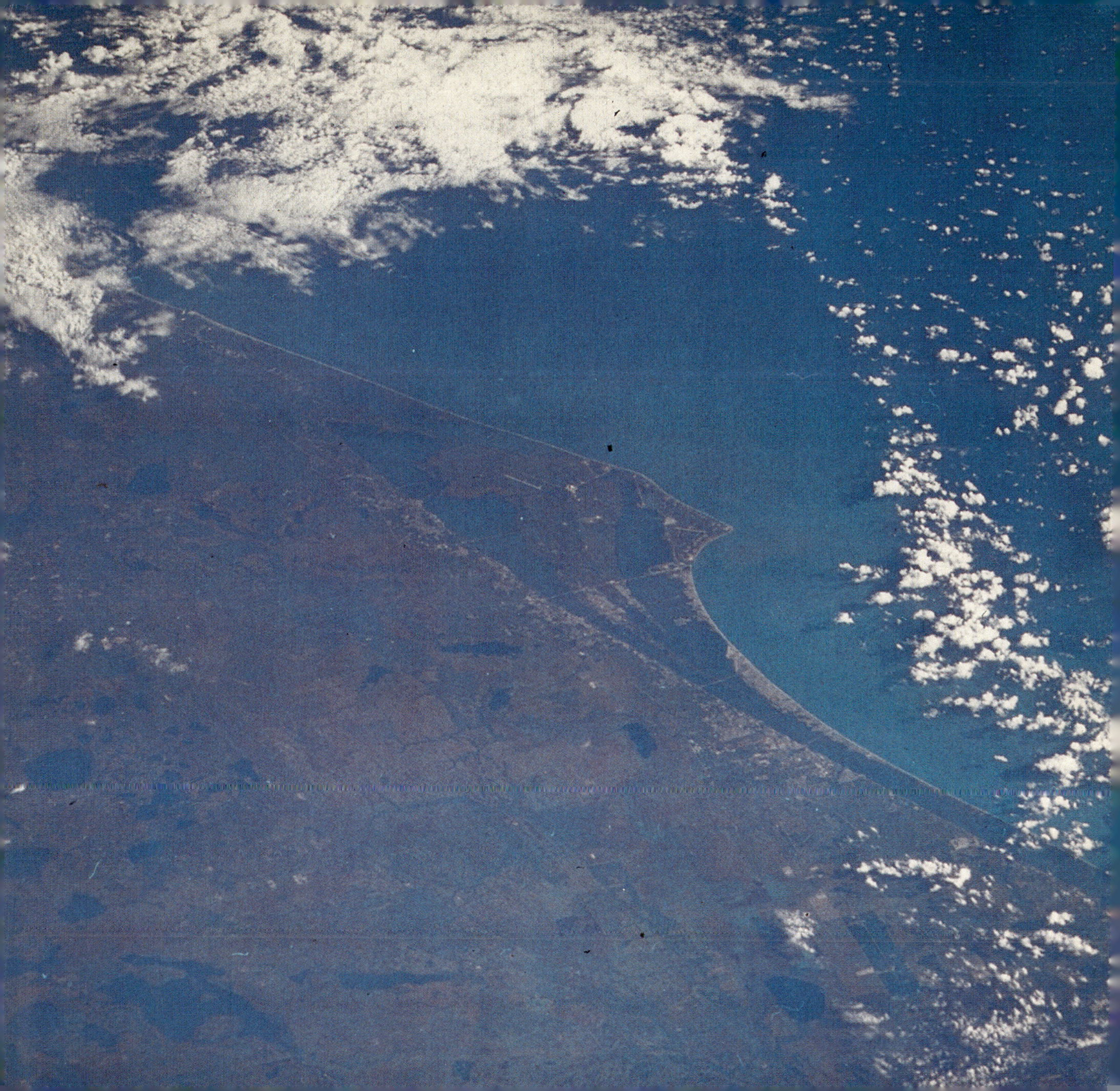

Landsat looks at the surface of the earth. It tells people the state of the land. Other satellites look at the sea. Together weather, land, and sea satellites keep watch on our planet. Sea or ocean satellites gather information for people working on the sea. Whether for sailing or for trade, information about the condition of the sea is vital.

Weather satellites like this collect data from little stations on the ground ▶

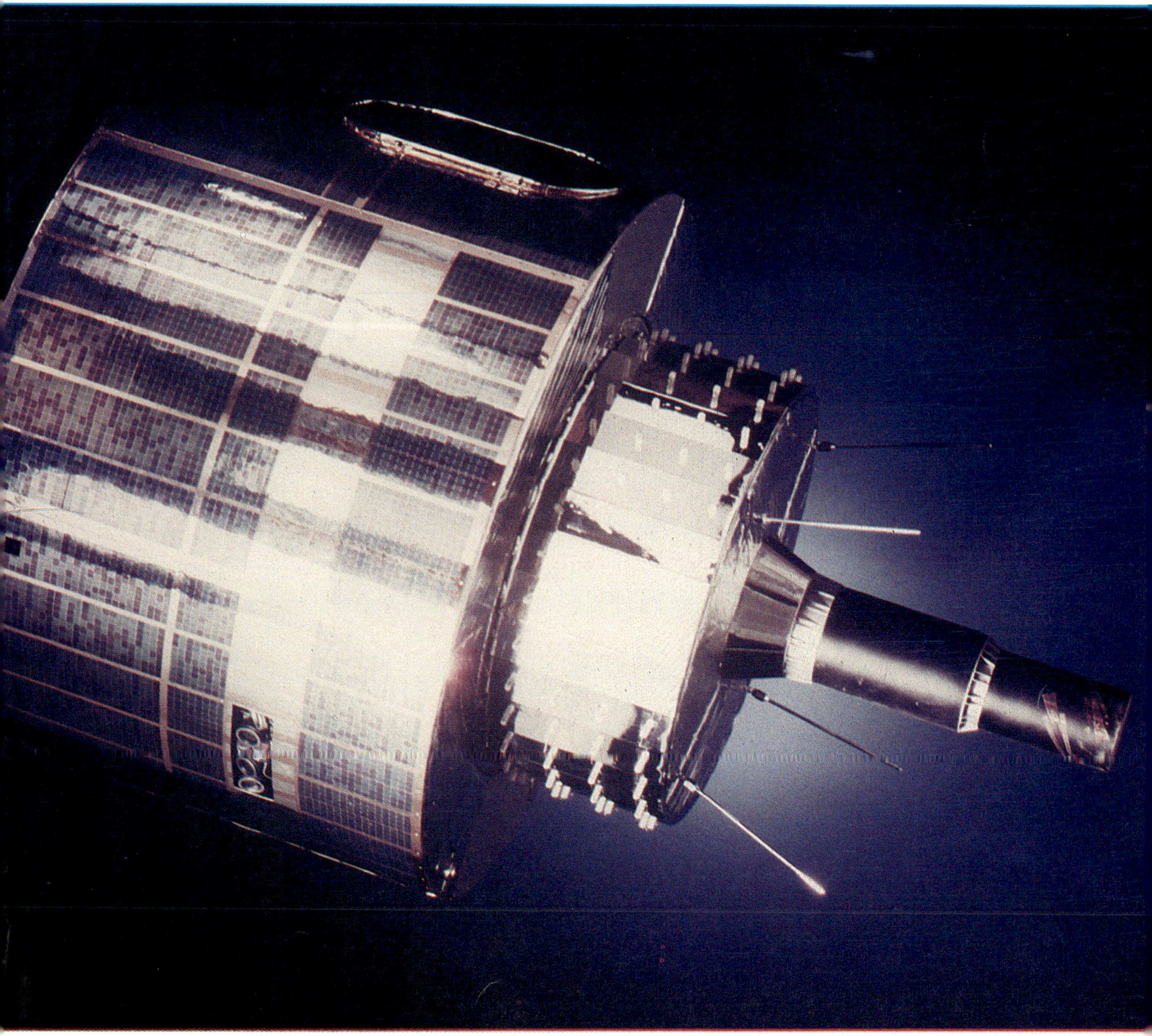

Satellites can help ship owners plan routes around bad conditions. They can also spot and track icebergs which threaten shipping. Most of the world's weather develops over the oceans. Because of this, meteorologists use satellites to track weather conditions at sea.

This view of the Nile River in Egypt helps scientists see how well crops are growing ▶

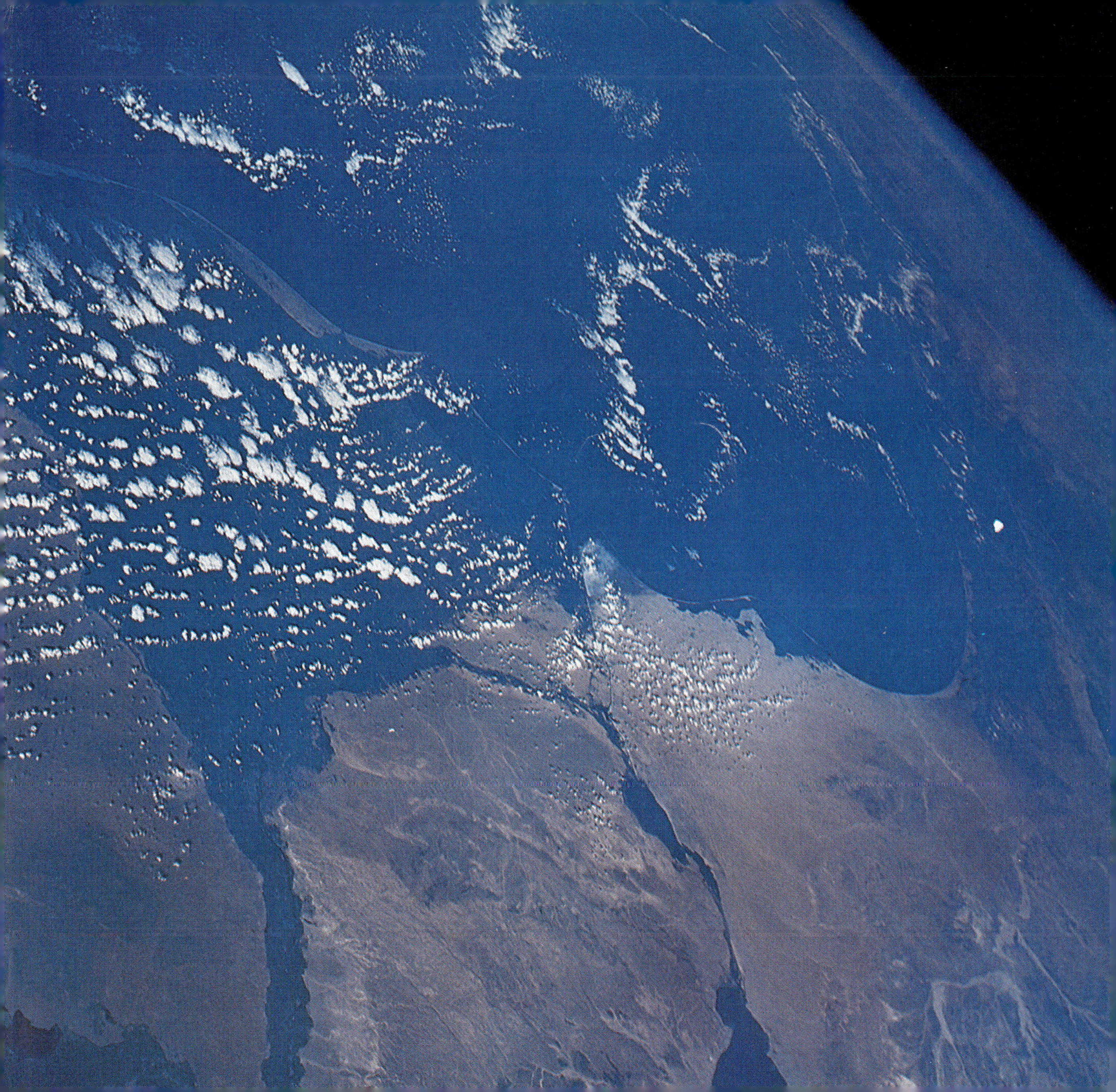

This information is also used to warn ships about storms, hurricanes or typhoons. When those violent disturbances come on land, weather satellites track their course. Since weather satellites were first used, many hundreds of thousands of lives have been saved around the world.

Satellites observe the desert to see where hidden wells of water might be found ▶

GLOSSARY

Data A series of measurements usually produced by a computer or computerized instruments.

Iceberg A large mass of ice floating in a sea or ocean.

Landsat The series of United States earth observation satellites used since 1972 for remote sensing of the earth's surface.

Meteorology The science of weather. One who works in meteorology is called a meteorologist.

Pollution A harmful substance, usually a chemical, which contaminates land, air, or water.